WORLD'S GREATEST BUSINESS PLAN THAT WORKS!

Acknowledgments

World's Greatest Business Plan was a challenging project due to its format, as I wanted a book that was simple and easy to follow. This meant a need for a graphic designer to work step-by-step with me through the entire project. This would allow me to make this *the most practical and easy-to-follow business plan book ever written,* so I want to thank my graphic designer who endured endless changes to get what I believe is the Greatest Business Plan in the world! So with that, I want to thank Michael Lovdal for all the assistance he provided.

Finally I want to thank my son Collin, who not only introduced me to social media, produces my podcast, assists with my platform but also endured listening to the endless changes and ideas I had for this book.

Download An Interactive PDF version of the business plan free at a secret link for World's Greatest Business Plan buyers only:

[See the PAGE 14 of this book!]

TABLE OF CONTENTS

BONUS CHAPTERS

1 Why Is This The Only Business Plan You Need?

Having just purchased and scanned through ALL the business plan books on Amazon's first page titled, *How To Write a Business Plan*, I was exhausted at their length, requiring countless exercises of no value.

> ***"By failing to prepare, you are preparing to fail."***
>
> *— Benjamin Franklin*

This business plan actually works and eliminates exercises that are purely a waste of time. For example, a financial projection, what you think your company will take in, is a fantasy. *This cannot be accurately projected by anyone.*

Having started more than 20 companies, I have never once had a projection that was anywhere close to what I thought we would generate. It was either more than I hoped for (which is great) or far less, which meant an adjustment needed to be made (and fast). I learned through 5 startups what I could plan for was: my startup costs—with some degree of accuracy—and my ongoing costs to operate the business. This is just one example of why this plan works and is simple but to be clear—it is *WORLD'S GREATEST BUSINESS PLAN!* Because it ***actually works***.

2 What is a Business Plan?

A business plan is a written document that describes in detail how a business—usually a new one—is going to achieve its goals.

> ***"A business plan lays out a written plan from a marketing, financial and operational viewpoint. Business plans are important to allow a company to lay out its goals and attract investment."***
>
> — *Investopedia*

A **business plan** is also a road map that provides directions so a business can plan its future and helps it avoid bumps along the road. It also can keep you from driving off the cliff of what is certain to be a bad idea that should not be moved forward on after the information revealed in your business plan.

What is a Business Plan?

WARNING!

I have personally been very excited about a potential business idea, but after the business plan prccess and specifically where I have done research on potential competition and pricing I have determined that the market was too crowded in my area or that the pricing could not be high enough to make the profit we would need to make for this to be an attractive venture.

Finally I have also had all signals pointing in the right direction and then when I was determining the WHO I would need to launch and operate this new business venture they were like trying to find a one eyed leprechaun. Hiring the talent was going to be near impossible for where I was located for what I needed again giving me the clear warning this was not a business I should move forward with.

Do not fall so in love with your business idea that you don't allow clear data that you find doing the business plan to alert you that your idea has weaknesses that should alarm and yes scream at you "this idea is not ready for the marketplace."

3 Why Do You Need A Business Plan?

GREATER CHANCE OF SUCCESS

Preparing a business plan has been proven to give you a greater chance of success.

> ***"A clear vision backed by definite plans, gives you a tremendous feeling of confidence and personal power."***
>
> *— Brian Tracy*

Palo Alto Software founder, Tim Berry recently reported on some new data showing the value of business plans. Palo Alto did a survey that asked thousands of its Business Plan Pro software users questions about their businesses, goals and business planning. The responses showed that *those who completed business plans were nearly twice as likely to successfully grow their businesses* or obtain capital as those who didn't write a plan.

Why Do You Need A Business Plan?

One study published in 2010 in the *Journal of Business Venturing* shared aggregated research on the business growth of 11,046 companies and found that planning improved business performance by 30%.

In a study highlighted in Entrepreneur by Mark Henriks to determine the value of a business plan, William Bygrave, a professor emeritus at Babson college, found a stunning conclusion—he found that *writing a plan dramatically increased the likelihood of someone actually going into business.*

In fact the conclusion was that you were, "two and half times more likely to go into business." The mere exercise and discipline required to write a business plan separates those who think they want to be an entrepreneur from those who will be an entrepreneur.

Finally, a study published in Small Business Economics found that entrepreneurs that take the time to create a plan for their business idea are 152 percent more likely to start their business. Not only that, those entrepreneurs with a plan are 129 percent more likely to push forward with their business beyond the initial startup phase and grow it. These findings are confirmed by another study that found that entrepreneurs with a plan are 260 percent more likely to start their businesses.

PROVIDES DIRECTION

The business plan is the blueprint for your business. If you wanted to build a house, you wouldn't walk over to an empty lot and just start nailing boards together. Starting a business without a business plan is just as foolish. As someone who has built homes, you begin with a clear picture of the end result as well as what will be needed to get you to this finished product. This will include all the people, supplies, permits, and order of events required to get this project done on-time and on-budget. Think the same way when constructing your business plan.

> ***"If you don't know where you are going, you'll end up someplace else."***
>
> *— Yogi Berra*

EXPOSES POTENTIAL WEAKNESSES

Venture capitalist and Silicon Valley pioneer Eugene Kleiner once stated that writing a business plan forces you into disciplined thinking. An idea may sound great, but when you put down all the details and numbers, it may fall apart.

It is far less expensive to find a flaw in your business idea before you go all-in. Don't be married to your business idea—allow it to be challenged by the business plan process as well as close trusted advisors.

> ***"An idea that has not been exposed to your critics is no idea that should be brought to the marketplace."***
>
> *— Sean Castrina*

4 Business Plan On A Napkin

Would it surprise you to learn that Southwest Airlines was started with a very crudely written **plan on a napkin,** outlining the idea for an intrastate airline? A pilot, Rollin King and attorney Herb Kellerman drew out a simple diagram that would resemble a triangle showing the flights needed to achieve this plan.

Oprah Winfrey, over dinner with movie critic Roger Ebert was introduced to a napkin business plan as well. Roger Ebert shared with Oprah the power in syndicating her daytime talk show laid out on a napkin. This plan would lead to her billion-dollar empire!

It's not the length of the business plan that makes it effective. It first must achieve one hurdle: Do you think this plan will work? Abraham Lincoln was once asked, "how long do you think a man's legs should be?" To which he replied, "Long enough to reach the ground."

THIS IS ALSO TRUE OF A BUSINESS PLAN.

It just needs to accomplish a few important things:

- Does it give you the **confidence** this will work?
- Does it give you a **detailed plan** to launch and operate this business successfully with **estimated costs**?
- **Who will you need** to successfully operate this business and what roles will they fill?

5 Know Your "Big 3"

1. INDUSTRY 2. CUSTOMER 3. COMPETITION

The more you know about the *Big 3* before going into business, the better.

Researching and understanding your *Big 3* will provide many answers required for your business plan.

Tell me about your industry:

HINT

What is it about this industry that you like?
Is it a growing or changing industry?
Are there any changes in your industry that you see are needed?

Tell me about your ideal customer:

HINT *(Be specific.)*

WARNING!

If you do not know your customer, you will never know their needs or how to best market to them.

Tell me about your competition:

HINT (Strengths and weaknesses.)

ADVICE› *If at all possible, do business with your competition prior to finishing your business plan. This will provide invaluable insight!*

WORLD'S GREATEST BUSINESS PLAN THAT WORKS!

Download An Interactive PDF version of this chapter free at this secret link for World's Greatest Business Plan buyers only:
WorldsGreatestBusinessPlan.com/download

PDF

INTERACTIVE

6 World's Greatest Business Plan

As the great football coach Herman Edwards famously shared, "You play to win the game." As an entrepreneur launching a startup, you have only 1 goal, TO SURVIVE. You learn to walk before you run and in the startup world, SURVIVAL is always goal number one.

1. WHY DO YOU WANT TO BE A BUSINESS OWNER?

HINT *Your why will motivate you when times are difficult so this needs to be strong and compelling.*

2. WHY DO YOU BELIEVE THIS BUSINESS IDEA WILL SUCCEED?

HINT *What about the initial idea appealed to you? Why?*

WARNING! *Support this with facts and data.*

FYI *This answer may change by the end of this business plan.*

3. WHAT RESOURCES DO YOU LACK TO LAUNCH AND GROW YOUR COMPANY?

HINT *Examples: Time, Expertise, Experience, Capital, Credit.*

THINK FURTHER› *How will you obtain these lacking resources?*

4. WHAT ARE YOU SELLING & WHY?

ADVICE› ***BETA TEST*** *to Confirm a Receptive Market.*

> ***"Life's too short to build something nobody wants."***
>
> *— Ash Maurya*

WARNING! ***42% of Startups fail because they do not meet a need.***
—CBINSIGHTS

People buy when you:

HINT

- Solve a problem that your customer believes is worth paying you to solve. (Examples: Trouble sleeping & snoring, home services, etc.)
- Meet a need (I need a car, I need groceries)
- Meet a want (I want a vacation, I want a BMW)

5. WHO IS YOUR COMPETITION?

THINK FURTHER

What do they do well? Where are they weak? How can you be different? Where can you be significantly better?

FYI *Competition is fine if you can be different or noticeably better.*

6. WHY WILL CUSTOMERS BUY FROM YOU OVER YOUR COMPETITION?

FYI *This is your **UNIQUE VALUE PROPOSITION**.*

HINT *Examples: Your pricing is better, you have faster service or deliver, a better / longer warranty, better selection, product has multiple uses.*

7. WHAT CAN AND WILL YOU CHARGE FOR YOUR PRODUCTS OR SERVICES BASED ON INDUSTRY AND COMPETITION?

HINT *This is why experiencing your competition is critical.*

8. WHAT WILL IT COST YOU TO PRODUCE AND PROVIDE WHAT YOU ARE OFFERING CUSTOMERS?

HINT *Examples: Cost of labor to provide a service, cost to produce or manufacture a product.*

9. WHAT ARE YOUR PROFIT MARGINS?

HINT *(Cost to Produce) – (Price Customers Pay) = Margin*

⚠ WARNING!

Remember this profit margin when you determine the cost to operate later in this chapter. The margin needs to be large enough to cover operating costs and provide a profit margin attractive to you AND potential investors.

"The most important thing to remember is you must know your audience." [Target Customer.]

— Lewis Howes

10. DESCRIBE YOUR TARGET CUSTOMER.

HINT *(Think like an FBI profiler: age, gender, single or married, etc.)*

FYI *Once you determine who your target customer is, this person is your* ***target market*** *(who you will put your marketing and sales efforts towards.)*

What is your potential market size?

HINT *Based on your target customer, how many of them are there in your area? How many of your target customers are searching for your product and services?*

What is the Lifetime Customer Value (LTV)?

HINT *This is the total money customers will spend over a LIFETIME with you.*

WARNING!

You don't want a business that has a one-time sales potential to its customer. (Unless you are selling high-priced items like yachts, islands, or jets.) Is your product or service something that your target customer will continually need?

11. CHOOSE A BUSINESS NAME

First Choice

____

Second Choice

____

Third Choice

____

⚠ WARNING!

- **Does it limit you?** (Geographically, generic, etc.)
- **It is confusing?**
- **Is it available?** (Check state corporation website.)
- **Can you get the domain for it?**

12. WHAT WILL I NEED TO GET THIS COMPANY OFF THE GROUND AND WHAT WILL THIS COST?

HINT

Examples: Bank Account, Merchant Services, Office equipment, Machinery, Equipment, Storage, Phone Service, Email set up, Website, Tech Support. What else?

FYI

This becomes a massive to do list with costs and deadlines. Your list will be unique to your business.

TO DO LIST

ITEM	COST	DEADLINE

ADVICE › *I suggest that you break up this massive list into daily chunks (in groups of similar tasks). Example all things money related (bank account, paypal, merchant services) then office set up, etc.*

TO DO LIST *(CON'T)*

ITEM	COST	DEADLINE

HINT *Examples: Office equipment, machinery, equipment, storage, phone service, email set up, website, bank account, merchant services, tech support, etc.*

13. PROTECT YOURSELF AND YOUR BUSINESS.

What insurance policies do you need to protect yourself and your business?

HINT *General Liability, Workers Compensation, Umbrella, Errors and Omission. What else?*

ADVICE› *Speak to a local reputable insurance agent that has experience working with startups and small businesses.*

WARNING!

Learn your state / area LABOR LAWS!

Are there any patents or trademarks you need to apply for?

Do you need any contracts and / or agreements?

HINT *Partnership agreements, NDA, Non-Compete, Employment. What else?*

14. HOW TO FIND YOU

- [ ] **Purchase a Domain**
  For YourBusiness.com

- [ ] **Get a Phone Number**
  (If Needed. Maybe a Toll-Free Number?)

- [ ] **Get a Mailing Address**
  (If Needed. Maybe a P.O. Box?)

- [ ] **Register an Email Address**

- [ ] **Register Social Media Accounts**

- [ ] ______________________________

- [ ] ______________________________

- [ ] ______________________________

15. MAKE IT OFFICIAL

- [ ] **Incorporate**
- [ ] **Business License**
- [ ] **Get an EIN at IRS.gov**
  (Employer Identification Number)
  https://www.irs.gov/businesses/small-businesses-self-employed/apply-for-an-employer-identification-number-ein-online
- [ ] ______________________________
- [ ] ______________________________
- [ ] ______________________________
- [ ] ______________________________

16. WHAT WILL THE ONGOING COSTS BE TO OPERATE THE BUSINESS?

HINT *Labor, production costs, insurance. What else?*

⚠ WARNING!

This list may grow as you answer additional questions.

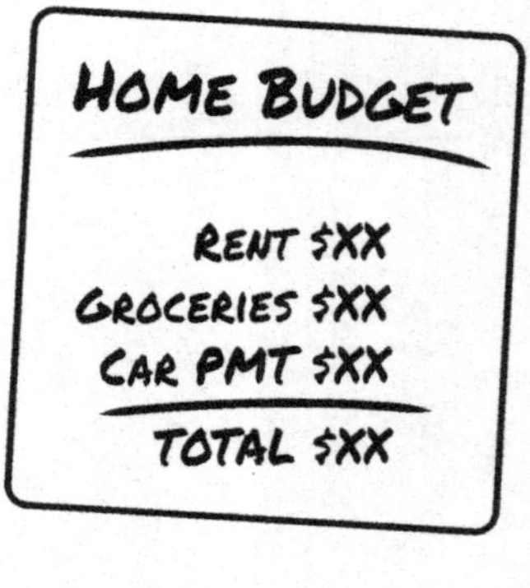

17. FINANCIAL PROJECTION

How long will it take to break even?

⚠ **WARNING!** *Be realistic based on conservative projections.*

What is your plan to get there?

____

____

____

____

____

____

____

____

____

HINT ***Burn Rate?*** *This is a number of how much capital you have versus how much it will cost to be in business. This gives you how long you can stay in business with no or limited new revenue coming in.*

⚠ WARNING!

Picture an oxygen tank on your back (similar to a scuba diver) and you start your business with a fixed amount of oxygen left over from your startup launch costs now every penny you spend moving forward causes you to have less oxygen for survival.

18. WHO WILL YOU NEED TO OPERATE THIS BUSINESS SUCCESSFULLY?

HINT *Examples: Who will open the door in the morning? Who will answer the phone & emails?*

> ***"The team with the best players wins."***
>
> *— Jack Welch*

FYI ***Good Sources for New Employees:*** *Indeed, Craigslist, LinkedIn, Zip Recruiter, Glassdoor, Monster, Ladders.*

Let's Pick Your Team

⚠ WARNING!

Run employment ads to determine how easily it will be to staff your critical needs to operate your business. I would also hold some interviews to get a better idea of the labor market, talent available and salaries/ wages required to obtain the staff you need.

Professional Needs

HINT *Examples: Accountant, bookkeeper, attorney, payroll company. What else?*

ADVICE

Think like a newly-elected President who is forming their cabinet. What trusted advisors will you need?

WARNING!

Hire proven, reputable, local professionals that you can sit in front of to talk with in person.

If you have no idea who to call, ask some local successful business owners who they recommend. Your chamber of commerce could also provide great recommendations.

19. WHAT WILL THE MANAGEMENT/LEADERSHIP STRUCTURE LOOK AND FUNCTION LIKE?

What will your role be?

How will the leadership structure look and function?

"The single biggest way to impact an organization is to focus on leadership development. There is almost no limit to the potential of an organization that recruits good people, raises them up as leaders and continually develops them."

— John Maxwell

> ***"A brand for a company is like a reputation..."***
>
> *— Jeff Bezos*

20. BUILD YOUR BRAND

What Is A Brand?

A brand is an identifying symbol, mark, logo, name, word and/or sentence that companies use to distinguish their product from others. A combination of one or more of those elements can be utilized to create a brand identity.

Legal protection given to a brand name is called a trademark. *Source: Investopedia*

Why Do You Want To Build A BRAND From Day ONE?

It will serve as the foundation of your marketing/ advertising efforts. By identifying what you want your brand to be as well as establishing the traditional pillars of a brand this will give you the direction needed to attract your target customer.

LOGO

☐ **Design a logo** that would best represent your company name and image.

⚠ **WARNING!** ***Have a professional graphic designer do this!***
See resources on page 133.

GOOD EXAMPLES:

FedEx

What examples, colors, or distinctive elements will you bring to your graphic designer for inspiration?

FYI ***Sketch your ideas out!***

BRANDING POSITION

This is what you want your customers to think of your company. You are placing an image in their mind when they hear or think of your company.

GOOD EXAMPLES:

VOLVO

Has take the brand position of **SAFETY** within the automotive industry.

ROLEX

Has taken the brand position of **TIMELESS QUALITY** within the watch industry.

BMW

Has taken the brand positioning of **"THE ULTIMATE DRIVING EXPERIENCE"** within the automotive industry.

Walmart

Has taken the brand positioning of **LOWER PRICES** and **SAVING MONEY**.

HINT

This should reinforce a quality or image that you want your customers to think of when they think of your company.

MY BRANDING POSITION IS:

____

____

____

____

____

____

Let me help you!

A simple but effective way to choose a very effective branding position is to ask, *"What one quality, promise or experience if we could deliver on would make our customers chase us down for our business?"*

TAGLINE

A catchy / memorable phrase that reminds customers of a unique quality or brand position you have claimed) that you can put under your company logo and name. This can also can and should be used in all your marketing material.

GOOD EXAMPLES:

Just Do It.

I'm Lovin' It!

Is It In You?

Open Happiness.

Think Different.

Because You're Worth It.

21. HOW WILL YOU ATTRACT YOUR TARGET CUSTOMER?

FYI *You are now developing your marketing plan.*

HINT *What advertising vehicles will be the most cost effective to reach your target customer? Example: Digital ads, social media, TV, radio, Direct Mail, affiliates, etc.*

WARNING! *Your goal is to reach the most target customers using the least amount of money.*

How does your competition attract their customers?

☐ **Digital Advertising**
(Display Ads, Programmatic)

☐ **Social Media**
(Facebook, Instagram, etc.)

☐ **Google**
(Organic SEO and Paid Search)

☐ **Streaming Video & Music Ads**
(Hulu, YouTube, Spotify, Pandora)

☐ **Influencer & Affiliate Marketing**

☐ **Radio**

☐ **Television**

☐ ______________________________

☐ ______________________________

☐ ______________________________

☐ ______________________________

THINK FURTHER

What do you like about their marketing?

What can you copy or emulate from their marketing?

What can you do that will be different and stand out?

DEVELOPING YOUR MESSAGE (TO YOUR TARGET CUSTOMER)

"Marketing is winning customers to what you're selling by sharing compelling reasons why they should love what you are selling."

— Sean Castrina

Is there a language (slang, cultural, age level, education level) you need to communicate?

If so, what 1-3 items can you communicate that your TARGET CUSTOMER would respond well to?

HINT

Company Qualities such as locally owned, made in the U.S.A. *(or whatever country or area would be applicable),* charitable participation *(example: Tom's Shoes or Bombas Socks who both donate a pair of shoes or socks for every pair purchased.)*

Competitive Advantages such as free delivery / returns, same day service, at store pick up, size of selections, pricing, etc.

Consider a CALL TO ACTION:

HINT

What would make someone buy today? You want to create urgency or scarcity. (Example: limited time offer, on Sale Today, limited supply, etc.)

ADVICE

Call to action is very effective when you can offer discounts, you have a sale or promotion.

> ***"Effective marketing is measured in massive customer acquisitions."***
>
> *— Sean Castrina*

Example of Your Completed Marketing Message:

____

____

____

____

⚠ WARNING!

BETA TEST*: Do a test in small samples to your target customer with various messages to see which message resonates or works best.*

Would Customer Testimonials Be Effective?
Yes or No?

ADVICE

If you are selling anything that has a history of skepticism (medicine, home services, financial service product. etc.) it is always helpful to have a real customer testimony that can share their positive experience. Is your product or service completely new? If so, testimonials are a great way to overcome skepticism and concerns.

HOW DO I GET TESTIMONIALS IF I HAVE NOT LAUNCHED MY BUSINESS YET?

ADVICE

Create a beta group of friends, family, co-workers, church members, neighbors who will try your product or service and share their feedback, comments and experience via written testimony, video endorsement, etc. that you can use in your marketing.

Is there a celebrity (actor/ athlete, recognized personality) that you could get to give your company/ product/ service instant credibility or massive recognition?

____

____

____

____

FYI *This is **INFLUENCER MARKETING.***

ADVICE

Do you have a local person that would be affordable or you could trade your products/service for their testimony? Is there a game changing celebrity/ athlete that would be worth paying a king's ransom, percentage of profit and possibly a share of ownership for their endorsement?

How to Create an Effective Customer / Celebrity Testimonial or Endorsement

HINT

Needs to be authentic (Will your audience believe what this person is saying?)

- Promote your Competitive Advantage
- Overcome skepticism
- Build Trust

ADVICE

You, the creator of the product or founder may be your best spokesperson. If you can communicate in a way that is receptive to your target audience—*DO IT YOURSELF.*

Media Ad Buy / Programming Considerations

HINT

Your target customer has programming that fits them best. Example: high income male customers tend to watch golf, so Sunday afternoon programming is effective.

PUTTING IT ALL TOGETHER

What message?

What messenger?

What vehicle? *(Digital ads,TV, direct mail, radio, etc.)*

What media programming is the best fit?

Don't forget your BETA TEST—test you message, messenger, vehicle, as well as programming in small increments to see which works best!

22. WHAT WILL MY SALES STRATEGY BE?

HINT

How will customers buy your product or service? Examples: Ecommerce, Salespeople, Affiliates, Retail, Direct Sales, Multi-Level Marketing, Memberships, Subscriptions, Click Funnel. What else?

23. WHAT ADDITIONAL OPPORTUNITIES DO YOU SEE FOR GROWTH?

HINT

Can you expand to additional locations?
Can you franchise this business model?
Can you offer additional services to your target customer?
Can you offer more uses of your products?
Can you expand your product line?
Can you sell your products in more stores or channels?
Can you offer affiliate sales opportunities?

24. ARE THERE ANY STRATEGIC PARTNERSHIPS, AFFILIATES, ASSOCIATIONS, AND ALLIANCES YOU CAN FORM OR JOIN AND IF SO WITH WHOM?

Are there association memberships that would give you credibility?

HINT *Industry associations, BBB, Builders Association, Influencers. What others?*

Are there strategic partnerships you could form?

HINT *Example: A new restaurant may partner with a reputable bakery or local farmers.*

FYI

CONGRATULATIONS!

You just finished a detailed

MARKETING PLAN.

(Questions 20–24.)

"Rule 1 in Business: Never Stop Acquiring Customers.

[Marketing] Rule 2: Never forget Rule #1!"

— Sean Castrina

25. BUSINESS STATEMENTS

MISSION STATEMENT

A Mission Statement is, "a written declaration of an organization's core purpose and focus that normally remains unchanged over time."

— *BusinessDictionary.com*

GOOD EXAMPLE:

goodwill

"Goodwill works to enhance the dignity and quality of life of individuals and families by strengthening communities, eliminating barriers to opportunity, and helping people in need reach their full potential through learning and the power of work."

GOOD EXAMPLE:

Microsoft

"Our mission is to empower every person and every organization on the planet to achieve more."

MY MISSION STATEMENT:

ADVICE

Try and answer these questions: Why are you in business? What will make you stand out to the customer?

VISION STATEMENT

A Vision Statement is, "an aspirational description of what an organization would like to achieve or accomplish in the mid-term or long-term future.

It is intended to serve as a clear guide for choosing current and future courses of action."

— *BusinessDictionary.com*

GOOD EXAMPLES:

goodwill

"Every person has the opportunity to achieve his/her fullest potential and participate in and contribute to all aspects of life. "

"Bring inspiration and innovation to every athlete in the world."

GOOD EXAMPLE:

Microsoft

"To have a computer on every desk and in every home."

My Vision Statement:

____

____

____

____

____

____

____

____

ADVICE› *Be concise, clear, timetable, future oriented, challenging and inspirational.*

VALUE STATEMENT

A <u>Value Statement</u> is, "a declaration that informs the customers and staff of a company's top priorities and what its core beliefs are.

These values will be demonstrated in the conduct of its employees.

Companies often use a value statement to help them identify with and connect to targeted consumers, as well as to remind employees about its priorities and goals."

— BusinessDictionary.com

GOOD EXAMPLES:

apto

"Be Remarkable, Take Ownership, Be Introspective, Be Uncomfortable, Execution Matters. "

L.L.Bean

"Treat your customers like human beings and they will always come back for more."

MY VALUE STATEMENT:

ADVICE› *Be authentic, with emotional appeal and link to expected conduct of employees.*

WARNING! *First time entrepreneurs: don't get trapped spending endless hours on this. This is a weekend project after you have done everything else.*

7 30-Day Startup Game Plan

I have always found any large or overwhelming project is simpler when you break it up into bite size chunks. As I have heard it said "How do you eat an elephant? One bite at a time." So what I wanted to do was break this business plan into an actual 30 Day Game Plan. This allows you to focus on one specific part of the business plan each day. This is a strategy I have used for years and works great for those who are currently working a full time job and do not have all day to work on this business plan:

Day 1

#1 Why do you want to be a business owner?

Day 2

#2 Why do you believe this business idea will succeed?

Day 3

#3 What resources do you lack (time, expertise, capital, skills, etc.)

Day 4

#4 What are you selling and why?

Day 5

#5 Who is your competition?

DAY 6

#6 Why will customers buy from you over your competition?

DAY 7

#7 What can and will you charge for your products or services based on your industry and competition?

DAY 8 (both 8 and 9)

#8 What will it cost you to produce and provide my offerings to my customers?

#9 What are your profit margins?

DAY 9

#10 Describe your target customer.

Day 10

#11 Choose a Business Name (was #16)

Day 11 and **12**

#12 What will you need to get this company off the ground and what will this cost?

My advice is to break this massive list into daily chunks (in groups of similar tasks). Example all things money related (bank account, paypal, merchant services) then office set up, etc.

Day 13 and **14**

#13 Protect yourself and your business

Day 15

#14 HOW TO FIND YOU

Day 16

#15 Make it official

DAY 17

#16 What will the ongoing costs be to operate the business?

DAY 18

#17 Financial Projection

DAY 19 (Both 18 and 19)

#18 Who will you need to operate this business successfully?

#19 What will the management/leadership structure look and function like?

Day 20 and **21**

Interviewing members who will join your team from staff as well engaging professionals (cabinet members) to work with you.

DAY 22

#20 How will you attract your Target Customer? This is your marketing plan.

DAY 23 and **24**

#21 Branding

Choose a logo that would best represent your company name and image?

Choose a Branding Position

CREATE A TAGLINE (From your Branding Position)

Day 25

#22 What will your sales strategy be?

Day 26

#23 Are there any strategic partnerships, associations and alliances you can form or join and if so with whom?

Day 27

#24 What additional opportunities do you see for growth?

Day 28 and **29**

#25 Business Statements

Day 30

Murphy's Law-Finish whatever you have yet to complete!

30-Day Startup Game Plan

1 #1	2 #2	3 #3
7 #7	8 #8+9	9 #10
13 #13	14 #13	15 #14
19 #18+19	20 	21 
25 #22	26 #23	27 #24

30-Day Startup Game Plan

4 #4	5 #5	6 #6
10 #11	11 #12	12 #12
16 #15	17 #16	18 #17
22 #20	23 #21	24 #21
28 #25	29 #25	30 Murphy's Law

BONUS CHAPTERS

TABLE OF CONTENTS

8 Can Your Business Plan Take A Punch?

IN CLOSING

Please remember, your business plan is not doctrine and far from infallible. It is a plan that has given you the confidence this business idea can work.

It should also provide a roadmap to the target you have set to produce a successful business.

However, NOTHING in the startup world goes as planned, so your ability to change directions and see opportunities that you never imagined is a critical survival skill you must learn.

> ***"Everyone has a plan until they get punched in the mouth."***
>
> *— Mike Tyson*

In an insightful article in Forbes, Paul Brown shares how he set out to write a book sharing successful business plans and came to a discovery:

"There was only one problem with the book concept. Most of the business plans had nothing to do with what the businesses eventually became.

People who said they were going to specialize in "developing new computer hardware" ended up in software, for example.

Companies that started with the goal of "serving the end consumer" became specialists in helping distributors. In a surprisingly high number of cases, what was in the business plan ended up having very little to do with what the (successful) company ultimately became."

> ***"Plans are of little importance, but planning is essential."***
>
> — *Winston Churchill*

My advice is to create and follow your business plan until change is needed. It will not always be obvious so your ability to identify when to adapt or completely change course will oftentimes determine the success or failure of your startup.

9 Pitching Your Business Plan To Investors And Partners

When pitching your business idea to a potential investor, focus on what they would want from this deal. Pitch your idea to people who would have an interest in your business succeeding.

They are either people who have money, (can afford to) and would like to make a nice return on their money. They have a history of investing in startups or are family / friends who love you enough to make this investment in YOU. *Yes, they do it for you so don't present an idea that you are not very confident will succeed or your next family reunion will be awkward.*

DON'T pitch ideas to family / friends who cannot afford to lose their investment! Startups are risky no matter how confident you are, so don't put someone's life savings at risk on your startup idea.

Think like an investor—what would you want to see and hear from someone wanting your hard earned money?

Be brief and to the point—display confidence, not arrogance. People invest in people they like and trust.

Trust is based on proposing a feasible and profitable idea that they believe you can make happen. They are investing in you and your leadership of this company as much as the idea itself.

BRIEF PROPOSAL FOR INVESTORS:

1. Product Demonstration with all supporting patents and trademarks.

2. Prove this is a profitable/feasible business idea with supporting information.

What are you selling? Why will customers buy? What size is your potential market? What is your strategy to reach you customers and sell them? Explain how you will be different from your competition? (Proof of Concept)

3. Financial Breakdown

Cost to Launch ____________________

Cost to Sustain ____________________

Cost to Provide Goods/Services ____________________

Profit Margin ____________________

4. What will they get for their investment?

Loan Interest ____________________

Loan Terms

____

____

____

____

Ownership % ______________________

Stock Shares ______________________

HINT

This is often referred to as the Executive Summary portion of a business plan. My experience is that banks don't invest in startups. They loan money to people who have credit and collateral.

Who Has Final Say ______________________

Ownership / Decision Maker Breakdown

____

____

____

____

⚠ WARNING!

Be prepared to defend your business plan very similarly to a doctoral dissertation, or even better, a cross examination by an opposing attorney.

Don't be defensive, be direct and just provide the answers with confidence based on the information in your business plan. Don't be surprised that they have found weaknesses you may not have thought of.

It is possible you may need to come back with a specific answer they have presented. In the end you will have a better business plan after exposing your plan to smart, cautious critics.

10 The 7 Biggest Mistakes Startup Founders Make

1. They **fall in love with their business idea** and don't allow it to be challenged by others.

2. They **delay the start** trying to get everything perfect.

3. They **don't make needed adjustments** when sales are slow and customer interest is low.

4. They **spend money on items not essential for survival.** (Only spend money on things that lead to more sales and satisfying customers!)

5. They **make bad hires** that don't contribute high value from day one. (Stay away from the tendency to hire friends and family.)

6. They **focus on organization and culture, not SALES.** (Companies go out of business for one reason 99% of the time—they run out of money because of poor sales.

7. They **fail to continue setting new challenging goals** for their company. (Companies that plan and review results regularly grow 30 percent faster!)

11 5 Golden Rules For A Successful Startup

1. TEST YOUR BUSINESS IDEA

If at all possible BEFORE even doing a business plan. Try selling it on a very small scale to see if it resonates with customers and if they will pay what you are asking. The fancy term for this is, "PROOF OF CONCEPT." I don't care if you sell your product at the county fair or online through a click funnel, but you need to get validation that you are on the right track.

2. BE A GREAT ENTREPRENEUR

Venture Capital companies invest in the person who brings them the business idea every bit as much as the actual idea itself. They know the value of leadership and the "it factor." Some people just have that charismatic energy and confidence that you know they will succeed. Becoming a great entrepreneur is a learned skill that you too can learn! Grow your leadership, communication, and sales skills. Whether it is selling your idea to investors or trying to recruit a superstar to join your startup team, you will always be leading and selling.

3. PARTNER WHEN YOU CAN

I have always said I would rather have 50% of a lot then 100% of a little. What do all these great companies have in common? Apple, Microsoft, Uber, Southwest Airlines, Disney, Berkshire Hathaway? I could go on and on... they all started as partnerships. One of the partners may be more well-known and charismatic then the other, but these companies required the talent and resources of 2 people to launch iconic companies. When do you partner? When you are lacking a critical resource needed to start and or grow your business. Start with this list: do you lack expertise, business experience, capital, or time? These are all good reasons to partner.

4. MAKE ADJUSTMENTS AS NEEDED

Starting a business is like flying a kite—it only takes one strong wind to bring it down. Be very alert to changes you may need to make! Don't cling to your business plan when something is not working.

> ***"Change before you HAVE to."***
>
> *— Jack Welch, Legendary CEO of General Electric*

5. GUARD CASH LIKE OXYGEN TO A SCUBA DIVER

Don't spend a dime on anything that is not needed . (50% of what you think you need for your startup is a waste!) Think like a minimalist for the first 2 years. If it does not increase sales, don't spend money on it.

12 Be a Great Entrepreneur

This chapter is designed to help you **BE A GREAT ENTREPRENEUR**. I share how you can personally grow or improve *THE 10 QUALITIES GREAT ENTREPRENEURS SHARE*.

What is it that allows some to start a successful business and then grow it exponentially while others fail to even launch a business, let alone grow one?

There are, in fact, *repeatable personal characteristics* that the most accomplished entrepreneurs all seem to share. And sadly, those who fail to achieve also tend to share consistent characteristics, such as: procrastination, lack of leadership, drive, and motivation.

The good news—not only will I share with you the qualities of great entrepreneurs, but more importantly—I'll reveal how you can improve these traits in your own life.

> ***"Give me someone with a clear vision, unbreakable determination, relentless energy, and a big dose of optimism and I will give you back a great entrepreneur."***
>
> *— Sean Castrina*

1. DRIVEN

The first step to success in any endeavor, whether in sports, business, or others, begins with the commitment to work towards a given achievement.

I will provide a more robust definition shortly but, for now, know that ***drive*** *is the genesis of achievement*. The entrepreneur awakes each morning with a burning desire to bring an idea, not yet more than a thought, into a functioning, profitable organization. This simple, but consuming thought creates a drive within this person that is *relentless*.

Dictionary.com defines "driven" as *"being under compulsion (desire or need) to succeed or excel,"* as in, "a driven young man who was fiercely competitive." It also defines "driven" as, *"Controlled or propelled by something specified."* An entrepreneur should want and work toward this descriptor, as it means he or she works relentlessly towards achieving a given goal. Entrepreneurs drive themselves harder and place greater demands on themselves than the average person. When you become driven and it permeates who you are, this quality will then define you—going from an *adjective* describing one of your attributes to a *noun* synonymous with *who you are*.

Drive has an "identical twin," found in *determination.* As synonyms, they can be interchanged to best describe the quality required to achieve something beyond average. Legendary baseball manager Tommy Lasorda says, *"The difference between the impossible and the possible lies in a man's determination."* The successful entrepreneur may start with an ambitious goal, but that is only the first step in the achievement process. The ambitious goal must be followed by the commitment (determination) to do whatever is required to reach each milestone.

Management consultant Scott Gould identifies drive as one of three keys to succeeding in business and life. He shares, *"Drive is an inner quality that many people lack. It is drive that makes a person not accept the status quo. It is drive that makes someone not want to be mediocre. Drive is a quality that few have."*

Businesses are often compared to sporting events and military operations (for good reason). Each of these three areas of endeavor has measurable objectives and uses similar terminology: ***What is your goal?***

Your passion? Your objective? Do you think it's going to be easy? If it was easy to obtain, why hasn't someone already done it? In fact, maybe right now someone out there has the same business idea you do and the difference between them getting that business up and running first and you being the victor is *how much you can drive yourself to cross the finish line.*

Are you so devoted to your goal or business idea that you are willing to sacrifice anything and everything in order to achieve it? Nick Woodman, the founder of GoPro, had the drive to create something and obsess over it until it became successful. *"He has a tremendous drive and presence, and when he says we're going to do something, I've come to believe it,"* says former Flextronics CEO and GoPro investor, Michael Marks.[1] Woodman was so devoted to making GoPro succeed that he didn't mind sacrificing other aspects of his life. He was quoted in Forbes as saying, *"I'll let myself obsess over things. To get GoPro started I moved back in with my parents and went to work seven days a week, 20 hours a day. I wrote off my personal life to make headway on it."*[2]

What goal so consumes you that you would pay a price in time, effort, ridicule, and more to achieve it? Bill Gates, Microsoft founder and (often) the world's richest man, admitted, *"I was quite fanatical about work. I worked weekends, I didn't really believe in vacations. I had to be a little careful not to try and apply my standards to how hard they (employees) worked,"* he said in an interview on BBC 4 Radio's *Desert Island Discs*. That fanaticism led him to track the comings and goings of employees so he could monitor just how much midnight oil they were burning. *"You know, I knew everyone's license plates so I could look out in the parking lot and see, when did people come in, when were they leaving,"* he said.

When you consider the daunting statistic that **half of all businesses fail in the first 2 years**, and then 9 out of 10 will cease to exist within a decade, you realize that you must be driven to succeed. B.C. Forbes advises, *"If you don't drive your business, you will be driven out of business."* To be driven, says Forbes, *"is the relentless pursuit of a goal without wavering, knowing the payoff will well exceed the price required to achieve it."*

What will drive you is pursuing a passion, not just money. Your passion may be an innovation or idea that you *must* see through to become a functioning organization. It may be the desire to build a team or have the profits you create serve as a catalyst for good. The reasons are endless, but personal financial success usually is not enough to will the entrepreneur to the finish line. Though money will be the by-product of achievement in business, it is usually *the last fruit to bloom* on the tree of a startup.[3]

What is the practical application to being driven as an entrepreneur? For one, you will never start a business without having the drive needed to complete all that is required to get an idea up and running—and operating for profit.

To succeed, you will have—or should have—defined goals that you are relentlessly pursuing within your business, from launching new products and services to new divisions and subsidiaries. Having ambitious goals and the drive to achieve them both attracts and retains high-level staff, as *everybody wants to work for a winner*. Jack Welch, G.E.'s CEO who grew the company's value by 4,000 percent, perhaps best expresses the connection between drive and this kind of successful leadership: *"Good business leaders create a vision, articulate the vision, and relentlessly drive it to completion."*

Any business desiring to grow and stand out will need in its leader someone with ambitious goals that ignite its followers.

How to be More Driven:

1. Find something worth achieving, where the sacrifice and effort is worth the payoff.

2. Begin with a one-year goal to achieve something with a payoff that motivates and, even better, *consumes* you.

3. Create 1-3 goals for your company, organization or division that, if achieved, would elevate your company to a new level.

4. Relentlessly pursue your goal. It often helps to break it into bite-sized (and measurable) pieces.

5. Begin developing this habit of setting and achieving goals, because in life and in business there will always be something worth accomplishing.

2. ENTHUSIASM

What is enthusiasm? Henry Ford provides a fine working definition: *"Enthusiasm is the yeast that makes your hopes shine to the start. Enthusiasm is the sparkle in your eyes, the swing in your gait. The grip of your hand, the irresistible surge of will and energy to execute your ideas."* Suffice it to say, if you have a few of those qualities, you might have some enthusiasm.

There is no real standard of measurement for enthusiasm, but most would agree it can be detected in those who have it. Bo Bennett is on the right track with, *"Enthusiasm is excitement with inspiration, motivation and a pinch of creativity."* You listen to a person when he talks, detect fire in his voice and conclude he is enthusiastic. You watch an aspiring entrepreneur share an idea or innovation and can *feel* whether or not her passion is revealed by enthusiasm. Investors can detect it, as can potential team members.

Elon Musk did not get to be worth $20.5 billion by being lackluster.[1] He exuded enthusiasm. At age 24, Musk dropped out of his Ph. D. program to become an entrepreneur in the areas of space travel, internet services, and renewable energy. He wasted no time—shortly after leaving school, he and his brother formed Zip2, a company that developed internet "city guides" for newspapers. Musk was key in obtaining contracts with The New York Times and The Chicago Tribune. When Zip2 was sold, Musk took his share of the money and invested in what would become Paypal. When eBay bought Paypal in 2002 for $1.5 billion, Musk again took his share of the money and invested in new ventures, the most notable of which were Tesla electric cars and SpaceX. Musk's enthusiasm is contagious. Everyone smiled when he put a Tesla into space using a SpaceX rocket. The Tesla is now orbiting earth—and being "driven" by a mannequin said to represent Musk.

Alexander Graham Bell is said to have been hardheaded, staunch, and not very interested in business. Perhaps if he had shown a bit more enthusiasm when he spoke those famous words, "Mr. Watson, come here—I want to see you." during the first telephone call, he would have had more investors and fewer lawsuits. Apparently he did not, and Western Union, a potential investor, was not impressed. An internal Western Union memo called Bell's invention, "a toy—idiotic, ungainly and impractical." When Western

Union later realized their mistake, they sued, saying Bell had stolen the idea for the telephone. Again, Bell's lack of enthusiasm came into play. He almost abandoned his invention, allowing Western Union and others to take his patents. Luckily, his partners did believe in the future of the telephone and would not walk away. At their urging, Bell filed his statement to the court just ahead of the deadline and retained his patents.[2]

The enthusiastic entrepreneur will often allow this trait to permeate all aspects of her business and this will create collateral success. Walter Chrysler defied his father's wishes that he attend college in order to work instead in a locomotive machine shop. His enthusiasm didn't go unnoticed and he consistently worked his way up the hierarchy within the railroad industry. Chrysler bought his first car, the Locomobile, in 1908. He didn't know how to drive, but that wasn't his first priority. He was fascinated by the mechanics and took his Locomobile apart and put it back together again.

When he was 35 years old, Chrysler met Charles Nash, then president of General Motors. Again, Chrysler's enthusiasm did not go unnoticed. Nash made him manager of Buick's factory. Chrysler initiated the assembly line process, thus tripling production. In 1915, he was made President of Buick. Under his leadership, Buick became the most successful brand in the country.[3]

Enthusiasm is one of the few things in business that will cost you nothing and requires no innate skill, but can be *learned in an instant and applied for a lifetime.* Let's look at just a few characteristics of this quality: The enthusiastic entrepreneur has passion evidenced by a contagious eagerness and excitement. Entrepreneur and business writer Jim Connelly shares, *"It's impossible to feel energetic and inspired about your business, unless you're enthusiastic".* Energy is the byproduct of enthusiasm. Says world soccer great, Pele, *"Enthusiasm is everything. It must be taut and vibrating like a guitar string."* Why would you not want this in your daily nature?

In what situations can enthusiasm be an asset to the aspiring entrepreneur?

- In acquiring new accounts, clients, and customers.
- In gaining a much-needed vendor, supplier or manufacturer.

- In assembling a team of employees.
- In recruiting a partner.
- In gaining favor with a bank or venture capital firm.

How to Grow Your Enthusiasm:

1. Get excited about things that excite you! Remember how you reacted at a concert or sporting event? Bring that type of excitement to your business and share your excitement with others.
2. Hire people that are naturally enthusiastic.
3. Minimize the negative people you choose to be around.

3. TAKING INITIATIVE

There is no substitute for the quality of taking initiative. Nothing can make up for the mistake of waiting for a good idea to become perfect. Taking initiative (action) on a good idea is much better than waiting for perfection. Hotel magnate Conrad Hilton observes, *"Success seems to be connected with action. Successful people keep moving. They make mistakes but they don't quit."* Taking action is the catalyst of all achievement.

The business world is filled with such examples. In the early 1960s, Ford Motor Company saw an opportunity to make an affordable sports car. In doing so, they followed General George Patton's advice: *"A good plan implemented today is better than a perfect plan implemented tomorrow."* The company took initiative and debuted the first Mustang at the 1964 *World's Fair* at Flushing Meadows, New York, five months ahead of the start of the 1965 production year. This bold initiative and follow-through resulted in more than 400,000 Mustangs being sold within the first year.

This move forced Ford's major competitor, General Motors, to quickly develop a performance automobile to attempt to compete with the Mustang. General Motors introduced the Chevrolet Camaro two years later. By this time, over one million Mustangs had already rolled off the assembly line and garnered a permanent fan base of both men and women drivers.[1] To this day, the Camaro has yet to catch up in overall sales during a near-50-year contest with the Mustang, and the Mustang has outsold the Camaro in 28 of the 36 years in which both cars were manufactured.[2] Larry Winget consolidates this principle into a short maxim: *"Implement now, perfect later."*

Although warfare analogies like the one from General Patton have since gone out of fashion in business school thinking, there is still a strong belief that the smart thing for a business to do is to look for *uncharted, currently non-existent markets where the water is blue and there is everything to play for.* The idea is to avoid shark-infested waters where late-comers are likely to be gobbled up in a feeding frenzy.[3]

Again, examples of where these insights have been proven in action in the real-world history of American business abound. Here are but a few:

- **Pandora** – which trailblazed the online music streaming industry, beating out Apple's iTunes successor by years.
- **eBay** – which was the first to implement an active online consumer auction process and popularized e-commerce.
- **Xerox** – which invented and (for 15 years) dominated the photocopying industry.
- **Coca-Cola** – which created the first cola-flavored soft drink.
- **Apple** – which was the first to introduce real touch screen technology to the masses.[4]

Be a Great Entrepreneur

The successful entrepreneur recognizes that *speed to market is critical*, which means that even when you have an idea, the quality of taking initiative is the next indispensable step. Without initiative, ideas sit dormant, never becoming what they could be. When you wait too long, your idea may even end up becoming someone else's great idea, as potential competitors may be (and likely are) close behind. The only difference will have been that they took action when you did not.

Tony Robbins, the motivational speaker and entrepreneur who parlayed his influence into a billion-dollar empire of business holdings, implores, *"Success comes from taking the initiative and following up—persisting."*

What simple action could you take today to produce a new momentum toward success in your life? The achiever takes strategic action daily. This does not mean action for the sake of action. There always needs to be a plan. But a perfect plan is not worth waiting around for.

One final plea for converts: *"Success comes to the person who does today what you were thinking about tomorrow,"* *—Anonymous*

How to Improve at Taking Initiative:

1. Recognize that being first has its rewards.
2. Recognize that moving forward on a good idea is better than waiting for a perfect idea.
3. Stop procrastinating in general. It will affect your leadership negatively.
4. Ask yourself what project or initiative you're currently considering would benefit from speedier action?
5. Determine what one initiative would have the highest payoff if you took immediate action on it and saw it through to completion.

4. FOCUS

How many people know that Steve Jobs spent FOUR YEARS cutting unsuccessful products, reducing costs, and improving operations with Tim Cook, Apple's COO (now CEO), before he ever released the iPod? He got EVERYTHING else out of the way before Apple could start innovating again, all for one CRITICAL reason: the need for FOCUS.

Focus is a guiding principle for the most successful entrepreneurs. Jobs identified "focus and simplicity" as one of his mantras, saying, *"Simple can be harder than complex: You have to work hard to get your thinking clean to make it simple. But it's worth it in the end because once you get there, you can move mountains."* As you set out to focus and simplify, know you have a challenge ahead. However, if you keep in mind the ultimate rewards, you'll be able to move through the process more easily and wind up with a well-oiled machine of a business.

By nature, entrepreneurs constantly brainstorm ideas and innovations, making it tough to know which deserve singular focus and which are better left unexplored. These determinations can feel incredibly high stakes, but they are necessary for an enterprise to thrive. Consider the wisdom of Entrepreneur.com contributor Steve Tobak: *"... more is never better. Better is better. And best is even better than that."*[2] Once you've embraced this philosophy, you can focus on the business of directing your business.

By saying no to all ideas but one, you build your brand; by building your brand, you create your business' future.[3] As tech startup success story Floyd DePalma notes, *"Chaos and the word YES create adrenaline. But clarity and the word NO create a true sense of purpose, bigger opportunities, more success and ultimately greater enjoyment in the work you do. The benefits are extraordinary."* [4]

Luckily, just as an athlete can train for a specific event or desired outcome, focus is a skill you can develop and improve. Oliver Kharraz, founder of Zocdoc, suggests this approach to stay focused: *"Pick something that you want to think about, and only think about that. Don't let anything else enter your thoughts. Try for five minutes in the beginning—and know that just like a marathon where you start with just a half mile to begin with, in the end you'll be able to do it for hours once you train for it."* [5]

The ability to focus is a critical skill for entrepreneurs, as you are constantly solving problems as well as creating new innovations; your to-do list is endless and completion of these tasks is not optional. Your ability to drill down deep on an idea or problem is a skill that can be learned—and can make the difference between success and failure. Pioneering motivational speaker and author, Zig Ziglar, implores, *"I don't care how much power, brilliance or energy you have, if you don't harness it and focus it on a specific target, and hold it there, you're never going to accomplish as much as your ability warrants."*

How to Improve Your Focus:

1. Try to remember a time or instance where you or your company were aiming for too many targets and hit none.
2. Prioritize what provides the greatest payoff for your time and attention.
3. Identify what has the highest payoff for your company's focus.
4. Begin spending time in silence, thinking and focusing on singular objectives.
5. Keep in front of you (in a banner, a journal, on your bathroom mirror) the project, initiative or goal that should be consuming your focus.

5. LEADERSHIP

Leadership! Every organization from sea to shining sea, including businesses, claims they need it, from Boy Scout troops, to the elite 82nd Airborne, to IBM, to the Salvation Army. The common denominator among all of these groups is that they are exactly that—*groups,* or more than one person. But leadership is not easily defined. Type, "define leadership" into Google and you get 338,000,000 hits. Look for books on the subject via Amazon and it will advise you that they have over 100,000 selections. *Popular topic, huh?*

You will never start and grow a business of any substance without the skill to lead others. I will take it a step further: you will not grow a durable business if it does not produce leaders from within. Great companies have a strong leader at the helm. The styles may vary, but these individuals guide the company toward the directions needed and withstand the storms of opposition that present themselves. But what they also do is create a system and culture where leadership is developed from within.

Why from within? Because team members inside the company know its culture and key initiatives. They are already on board. Trying to staff leaders from outside your organization is not only expensive, it takes much more time to get an outsider to understand how you operate and what values you prioritize.

Be a Great Entrepreneur

Leaders make decisions that have the *greatest consequences*. Then, at the helm, they set the priorities and initiatives they believe will have the *highest payoff*.

During the early 1980s, Jack Welch, CEO of General Electric, erased nine layers of management, demanded that business units be number 1 or 2 in their industry (or face being sold), and reduced the payroll from 411,000 to 299,000 employees. The ax he used to cut staffing was to lop off the bottom 10% of performers each year. When he took the helm in 1981, GE's revenue was $27 billion and its market cap was $14 billion. When he stepped down in 2001, revenue was $126 billion and the market cap was $400 billion.[1]

Leadership means making the critical decisions that dictate the death or survival of a company. It requires confidence in your ability to steer a business through change as well as turmoil.

"I've seen my share of boiled frogs," says Doug Yakola, comparing companies in crisis with the metaphorical frog that doesn't notice the water it's in warming up until it's too late. As the chief restructuring officer or CFO of more

than a dozen companies in turnaround situations over nearly two decades, Yakola has witnessed firsthand how managers back right into a crisis without recognizing that their situation is worsening. *"They're not bad managers, but they're often working under a set of paradigms that no longer apply and letting the power of inertia carry them along."* And if they don't realize they're facing a crisis, they won't know that they need to undertake a turnaround either.[2]

Inertia—in layman's terms, "If I ignore it will go away"—is too often the strategy for weak or inexperienced entrepreneurs. Brian Tracy, the author of over 70 books on self-development, reinforces this thought: *"Leaders think and talk about the solutions. Followers think and talk about the problems."*

You will need to be decisive as a leader. Nobody wants to follow someone who cannot make a decision. You will need to see into the future, making decisions where the answer will not be clear, such as what opportunities should your company take advantage of, as well as those it should pass on. You cannot become paralyzed when an important choice presents itself. Peter Drucker shares, *"Whenever you see a successful business, someone once made a courageous decision."*

At some point, the very survival of your business will require you, the leader, to chart a new course or to overcome a threat to your organizational survival. Former Vice President Dick Cheney warns, *"Direct threats require decisive action."* Your ability to recognize that a decision needs to be made NOW and cannot be delayed will be critical.

Together, these points create your three-step formula for beginning your leadership journey. To know the way, you need experience and expertise—this takes time but can be learned. Lead by example. And finally, show young potential talent how they can take the reins from you. At worst, they can hold the reins with you and having a team of strong and capable leaders is a credit to anyone who assembles and develops such a group.

How to Improve Your Leadership:

1. Accept that it is your responsibility to be a leader if you are starting, managing, or leading a business.
2. Read books, listen to podcasts and take seminars on leadership. Leadership can be learned and improved on.
3. Lead with your own style. Be authentic. You do not have

to be loud or *in-your-face* to be a great leader. You need to learn how to be yourself and still be able lead others.

4. Do not ignore problems or critical decisions. Be decisive!
5. If needed, or if you are new to leading, hire or partner with someone who can assist you in critical areas.

6. PERSISTENCE

On May 13, 2017, Martin Casado addressed the graduating class of his alma mater, Northern Arizona University. His opening words were probably a surprise to them. First, he told them, *"You are not going to meet your objectives."* Then he added, *"You are going to fail."* Not exactly the normal rousing speech given to a graduation class. He elaborated, saying, *"I only found computer science because I couldn't hack it as a physicist, and then I failed as a microbiology student. I made many, many missteps as the first-time founder of a company."* Nevertheless, Casado sold that company in 2012 for $1.26 billion. How's that for a guy who describes his vocation as his third choice? Pretty darn good for someone who admits to several bouts of failure.

We love stories of people who make it big in the marketplace. We generally define those who succeed as people who start a business that makes them a lot of money. But let's remember, roughly 90% of start-ups fail![2] This doesn't necessarily mean those who failed had a bad idea or were poor business people. Many factors could have caused their demise. Circumstances we cannot control play a role in the success—or failure—of our businesses. We can all remember vividly the effects of the Great Recession, during which over *170,000 businesses failed*.

If you've created a business that is humming along nicely, with balance sheets solidly in the black, congratulations! However, if you ever get knocked down, the only fix is to get up and try again. That's persistence! A business' failure is certainly not a desired outcome, but, statistically, you're far more likely to fail than to succeed. If that does happen to you, never giving up is what really makes the difference between an enduring failure and a temporary setback. Winston Churchill advised, *"Success consists of going from failure to failure without loss of enthusiasm."* Persistence! When one way doesn't succeed, find another.

In his book, *Failing Forward*, author John Maxwell takes on the subject of failure and provides a new paradigm for thinking about it. He lends this wisdom: *"Fail early, fail often but always fail forward."* This is what all successful people, including entrepreneurs, do. Failures are baked into the cake of life, but we must learn from our mistakes, gaining insight and clear direction, and allowing the lessons learned to become a catalyst for our eventual triumph. On a panel at the 2009 *Grace Hopper Celebration*, Nora Denzel, SVP of Intuit, advised prospective entrepreneurs to envision their career not as a "path" but an "obstacle course." If you expect the obstacles to come and see them as part of the journey, you will not feel daunted by them.[3]

A 2017 article in Small Business CEO, *The Importance of Persistence in Business,* points out that many companies fail because the owners and the main decision makers in these organizations give up too easily and prove unwilling to go the extra mile to make their businesses a success.[4] It's the business leaders who face their fears and the obstacles in their way head-on who eventually establish and grow the most profitable and effective businesses. Market leaders in any industry are typically those who are more innovative and enjoy taking on new challenges. By viewing obstacles that stand in their way as challenges, such companies demonstrate a belief that no business problem is impossible to overcome.

And let's not forget the famous persistence of *"The Colonel,"* who was told *"no"* 1000 times. Colonel Sanders was 65 when he decided he would begin to sell his fried chicken with its unique recipe. Sanders drove around the US in his white suit, knocking on doors and sleeping in his car. But it wasn't until 1964, at the age of 90, that Sanders finally sold Kentucky Fried Chicken to a group of investors for $2 million, which is $15.3 million in today's dollars.

The list of those who converted failure into success is nearly endless, because failure provides the crucial experience in learning, persevering, and finally launching the success of those who choose to never give up. Every great entrepreneur has a failure he can share. In those stories, you will hear lessons learned and innovations discovered that became part of the genesis that would take these people further than they had ever imagined. Napoleon Hill, the highly influential author of *Think and Grow Rich*, cements the subject with, *"Patience, persistence, and perspiration make an unbeatable combination for success."*

Dan Pink has famously said that *"persistence trumps talent."* Thankfully, you can learn to be persistent.

Talent often is something one either has or does not have in a given area of endeavor. The ability to never give up is learned; it is a mindset that can be adopted. And it is the bedrock of all successful people.

How to Grow in Persistence:

1. Decide now not to quit on something you are determined to accomplish.
2. Recognize persistence has a payoff—SUCCESS!
3. Understand that persisting in the little challenges will lead you to becoming persistent in areas of greater importance.
4. Look back to something you once quit from where you now wish you had persisted.

7. RISK TAKERS

Walt Disney once said, *"All our dreams can come true—if we have the courage to pursue them."* Let us unpack this truth further. Other words for courage include: daring, risk-taking, and adventurousness. To achieve anything substantial, you must make a bet on yourself. It only takes a glance at the annual Forbes list of the 400 Wealthiest Americans to see that entrepreneurs overwhelmingly dominate the list. A spot in the top 100 has yet to be attained by a doctor or lawyer.

The very definition of an entrepreneur is a person taking on financial risk. One entrepreneur who comes to mind for this trait is Elon Musk. At one point, after the sale of his shares in then-start-up PayPal, Musk had $200 million in cash. Back in 2010, he invested every last cent of this into his new businesses, leaving him personally broke—or, actually, *asset-rich* and *cash-poor*. Says Musk, *"My proceeds from PayPal were $180 million. I put$100 million in SpaceX, $70 million in Tesla and $10 million in Solar City. I had to borrow money for rent."* Now that's putting everything on the line!

Entrepreneurs often face this kind of dilemma, but Musk put even more on the line, borrowing money from friends to cover his day-to-day expenses—to the tune of $200,000 a month. And this was at a time when there was no guarantee of success for Tesla, as it wasn't until 2015, when the company received sizable government grants, that the tide turned for his company. It comes as no surprise that Musk has said, *"Take risks now and do something bold... you won't regret it."*[1]

We tend to view risk-taking negatively, often regarding it as dangerous, even unwise. But while some risks certainly don't pay off, it's important to remember that some do. Re-framing risk as an opportunity to succeed rather than a path to failure is something Sandra Peterson, CEO of the$10 billion business Bayer Crop Science, knows well. She told Forbes in 2011, *"Most women I know who have been successful in business, it's because they've been willing to take on the risky challenge that other people would say, 'Oh, I'm not sure I want to do that.' If you look at my career, I've taken on a lot of risky roles. They were risky to some people, but to me it was, 'Wow, this is great!'"*[2]

Not that entrepreneurs don't hesitate or have feelings of trepidation. It is normal—and healthy—to have some misgivings about risk-taking. But to be successful, they must look past their fears to the end result of their hard work, to the feeling of having a vision realized. As business coaching firm Action Coach reveals, *"Entrepreneurs are not immune to fear. But they prioritize their approach to life so that the fear of failure, frustration, boredom, drudgery and dissatisfaction far outweighs the lingering fear of success."* [3]

As entrepreneurship consultant and Babson College

professor Leonard C. Green always tells his students, *"Entrepreneurs are not [just] risk-takers. They are calculated risk-takers."* According to Green, calculated risk-takers are those who move forward toward their goals, keeping their eyes open and finding *"ways to reduce risk as they move forward with their businesses."* [4] This final piece is so important: **Successful entrepreneurs take a calculated risk wherein success for them is probable, but not guaranteed. —where the payoff is far greater than the sacrifice.**

How to Improve at Risk-Taking:

1. Take a Risk (where the payoff is worth it).
2. Learn how to get the odds of success in your favor (due diligence, partnering, etc.)
3. Be careful about going all-in. This will keep the risk from being catastrophic.

8. SELF-CONFIDENCE

Self-confidence is an inner belief a person has in himself and his abilities. It is not a fake bravado but a central nerve that allows such people to believe in themselves, their ideas and their ability to turn their objectives into reality. Some people exude confidence; you can feel it radiate as they step up to a podium, speaking with a voice of authority and a vocabulary that inspires an audience. It can also be displayed more subtly, but is still easily recognized when such individuals are making and explaining a difficult decision. Regardless of their unique styles, self-confident people are at their best when events are exceptionally trying. The self-assured person attracts others to join and assist her in her quest.

Business coach Cena Block says, *"Confidence ultimately is one of the key distinguishing factors in the level of accomplishment that individuals ultimately realize."* Block doubles down on that, saying, *"The secret weapon that distinguishes those who succeed from those who fail is none other than self-confidence."* The tendency for leaders to display confidence, which often is seen as extreme optimism, is supported by a study by the Kauffman Foundation on behalf of LegalZoom, which concluded, *"Ninety-one percent of entrepreneurs are confident that their businesses will be more profitable in the next 12 months."*

The entrepreneur, when infused with a startup idea, will hear countless times from naysayers that his idea will 'never work.' However, the self-confident pioneer of an idea will move forward with relentless optimism, knowing he can and will make it happen. To the person who does not possess this trait, succeeding in nearly anything will be unlikely, as it is hard to persevere in anything worth achieving if you do not believe you have the ability.

Steve Jobs and Steve Wozniak were just two geeks who happened to be friends. As young men, they were interested in computer technology, so they built a computer of their own. They were confident that they could make a computer more user-friendly to the average person. They added a keyboard to their machine and modified a small home television set so that it could be used as a monitor. They were confident that their computer would someday be a staple in every home, despite naysayers who argued there would never be a use for home computers. One such pessimist was Ronald Wayne. A friend of Jobs and

Wozniak, Wayne owned 10% of the company when in was founded. Less than a month later, he lost confidence in the product and sold his share back to Jobs and Wozniak for $800. Wayne lacked the trait of confidence, and thus he lost what would be worth $72 billion today.[1]

Another secret to feeling and exercising self-confidence is to *stay within your strengths*. Know your weaknesses and seek to stay where you have your greatest competence. It is hard to be confident in an area you are weak or have little experience in. As you accomplish one achievement after another, your self-confidence will only grow. This will provide a 'hall of fame' of accomplishments you can draw on to gain confidence for new and challenging endeavors. Finally, I have learned, *"Show me a man with no confidence and I will show you a loser every time." — Sean Castrina*

How to Grow in Self-Confidence:

1. Keep a journal of your own past achievements that you can regularly reflect back on.
2. Associate with people who believe in you and verbalize it.
3. Associate with those who have a positive view of things.
4. Receive coaching or mentoring to build your belief in a key needed area of strength.

5. Try self-talk. This is your inner dialogue. When you talk to yourself, affirm your positive qualities.

9. TEAM BUILDERS

On December 1, 1913, Henry Ford installed the first moving assembly line for the mass production of an entire automobile. His innovation drastically altered the time it took to build a car, reducing the process from more than 12 hours to only 2 hours and 30 minutes.[1]

The implementation of the assembly line shows Ford understood the value of building a team. And he reaped the spoils of that understanding. His earnings reached their pinnacle in 1920, when, at the age of 57, a Forbes magazine cover proclaimed him the World's Wealthiest Person; his net worth when he died in 1947 was a staggering $188 billion (adjusted for inflation).[2]

Apple co-founder Steve Jobs lays the foundation for understanding this elite entrepreneurial trait when he says, *"Great things in business are rarely done by one person. They are done by a team of people."* The list of legendary companies that started with a partnership — that is, a team —is eye-catching. It includes: Apple, Microsoft, Disney,

Hewlett Packard, and many more. These companies each had strong front-men, but their partners brought indispensable contributions to the table as well.

Leaders understand that two is often better than one; this reflects the beginning of understanding the value of surrounding yourself with other people who want to help you succeed. Gifted entrepreneurs are like a magnet for talent. In the beginning, these pioneers rarely have the funds to hire who is needed to scale their idea. So they share their idea like evangelists, converting people to join them and participate in their mission. Billion-dollar companies may begin with the vision of a single individual, but it takes a team of people with talent and determination to make that vision a reality. Carefully cultivating a tenacious and diverse team is essential to creating a large and successful company. In fact, it's sometimes said that hiring great employees is the single most important thing a founder can do. As business writer Drew Hendricks says of elite entrepreneurs, *"They realize that it's not a one-man show and that they have to surround themselves with talented, like-minded people to fill in the gaps."* [3]

Recruiting team members who *click* is like putting together a puzzle—you have to see the bigger picture to understand how the individual pieces fit. The effort you put into this process will be worth it. An effective team will be an unstoppable force that will drive your organization's success over the long term.[4]

Leaders of successful startups master three phases of Team Building:

1. **Hire the right employees.** Winners know how to find, select, hire, train, motivate, reward and retain great employees. They thoughtfully eliminate workers who don't contribute.[5] They elevate those who do and assemble the best team possible. As Bill Gates has described regarding Microsoft, *"If we weren't still hiring great people and pushing ahead at full speed, it would be easy to fall behind and become a mediocre company."* One of the most critical aspects of growing any business is employing the right people. Get it right, and your business's growth trajectory is likely to continue or accelerate. Get it wrong, and each of your tentative steps forward might lead to a proverbial three steps back.

As Jonathan Jordan notes, *"It's costly, stressful and time-consuming to manage the consequences of a wrong hire."*

2. **Value employees.** Business winners also know how to keep employees happy and productive. Renowned business builders carefully watch over their employees like a shepherd over a beloved flock. They are kind, respectful, encouraging—and highly supportive. This unique attribute can be one of the most useful and powerful characteristics of an award-winning entrepreneur.

3. **Establish a winning culture.** According to Simon Sinek, best-selling author and influential thinker on successful team building, *"Customers will never love a company until the employees love it first."* [6] Successful entrepreneurs know that shared values, philosophies, and behaviors align and combine to determine the future success of an enterprise. They establish a positive culture that inspires and motivates workers.

How to Become a Better Team Builder:

4. Recognize that you need help to build anything great.
5. Acknowledge and accept your weaknesses.
6. Hire and partner with people who are strong where you are weak.
7. Know all the key positions that you need to fill.
8. Create a culture of excellence and fun.
9. Reward and develop team members.

10. SMART

"A smart man [woman] makes a mistake, learns from it, and never makes that mistake again. A wise man finds a smart man and learns from him how to avoid the mistake altogether."

— Roy H. Williams

Let me be clear, smart has nothing to do with education, as the Forbes top 10 list of wealthiest Americans is dominated by those who *did not finish college*, however they had business intelligence. They quickly identified opportunities that could and would become profitable. They were also smart enough to *know what they did not know* and often either partnered with someone or surrounded themselves with a team of experts. Being smart is oftentimes knowing what you don't know.

Smart entrepreneurs also have the *foresight* to see threats that can put them out of business and make company saving pivots that allow for survival. However, the hardheaded (lets call these people the dumb entrepreneurs), not only do not recognize threats to their business, they fail to make the needed changes for survival.

Veteran entrepreneurs, to achieve this title alone, must have learned the necessary lessons that failure teaches. The seasoned founder has made mistakes along their journey but has more importantly learned from these mistakes and has allowed them to be pillars of knowledge used in future successes. Failures I have often shared is the scar tissue of success.

The entrepreneur has a voracious appetite for learning as it has been said that Warren Buffet, famed investor, spends 80% of his day reading. Bill Gates never heads out on a trip without his assistant loading his travel bag with no less than 10 books to read and finally billionaire Shark Tank star Mark Cuban has spoken of reading 2-3 hours each day. Do you see a pattern developing? The average CEO reads 60 books per year where few people will ever read another book following their formal education. You must choose to be a lifelong learner deciding to daily improve. At a minimum commit to better understanding business in general, leadership and the industry you serve.

I like to share that "failure is best learned through a second hand story' and books allow you to read and learn about the failures of iconic business leaders of the past and present. With today's technology where you can listen to podcasts and books with a simple app on your phone. Not to mention the endless webinars that are available with a simple click of your mouse. There is no excuse to not be a lifelong learner.

I encourage you to commit to becoming SMART, yes business smart, Become hyper alert to opportunities as well as threats to your business. Grow your area of expertise. This will require a commitment to daily learning. Where you lack expertise and experience be wise enough to surround yourself with those who do bring these components. And finally learn from every setback knowing the lesson will pay itself back with dividends in time. Finally lets learn a final lesson from Bill Gates, "Success is a lousy teacher, it seduces smart people into thinking they can't lose..."

Let's Review Why YOU Need to be Smart

1. See opportunities faster.
2. Decisive (based on confidence in your judgement).

3. Create and execute a plan.
4. Smart people attract smart people.
5. Innovative by nature.
6. See changes needed before the competition.

How to Grow Smarter:

1. Appreciate intelligence and expertise.
2. Recognize SMART has a payoff.
3. Read, attend seminars and listen to podcasts on your area of interest and strength.
4. Recognize you can't hide stupid. At some point your lack of knowledge will cost you.

Resources

Employee Identification Number
Interal Revenue Service (IRS)
irs-ein.tax.id.com

Domains
GoDaddy
godaddy.com

Digital Marketing
Includes Website Development, SEO, Online Presence
Gig Strategic
gigstrategic.com

Graphic Design
Logo, Style Guide, Social Media, Book Design
Michael Lovdal Marketing & Design
michaellovdal.com

Sample Business Plans
Bplans
bplans.com

Basic Legal Services
For basic contracts, agreements and incorporating.
Legal Zoom
legalzoom.com

Payroll
Paychex
paychex.com
Paycor
paycor.com

Banking

Always use a *local* bank that you can talk face to face with a loan officer.

Job Sites for Hiring

Indeed.com
Craigslist.com
Monster.com
LinkedIn.com
Glassdoor.com
ZipRecruiter.com
Ladders.com

Merchant Services

I recommend you use whoever you are banking with for your company.

Patents and Trademarks

U.S. Patent & Trademark Office
usa.gov/federal-agencies/u-s-patent-and-trademark-office

Uniforms

Cintas
cintas.com

Volunteer Business Consulting

SCORE
score.org

Download An Interactive PDF version of the business plan free at a secret link for World's Greatest Business Plan buyers only:

[See the PAGE 14 of this book!]

Endnotes

Brinckmann, J., Grichnik, D., & Kapsa, D. (2010). *Should entrepreneurs plan or just storm the castle? A meta-analysis on contextual factors impacting the business planning–performance relationship in small firms.* Journal of Business Venturing, 25(1), 24-40. doi: 10.1016/j.jbusvent.2008.10.007

Ding, E., & Hursey, T. (2010). *Evaluation of the effectiveness of business planning using Palo Alto's Business Plan* Pro. Department of Economics. University of Oregon.

Burke, A., Fraser, S., & Greene, F. J. (2010). *The multiple effects of business planning on new venture performance.* Journal of Management Studies, 47(3), 391-415.

Hechavarria, D. M., Renko, M., & Matthews, C. H. (2011). *The nascent entrepreneurship hub: Goals, entrepreneurial self-efficacy and start-up outcomes.* Small Business Economics, 39(3), 685-701. doi: 10.1007/s11187-011-9355-2

Liao, J., & Gartner, W. B. (2006). *The effects of pre-venture plan timing and perceived environmental uncertainty on the persistence of emerging firms.* Small Business Economics, 27(1), 23-40. doi: 10.1007/s11187-006-0020-0

Businessdictionary.com

Investopedia.com

Endnotes

REFERENCES FROM CHAPTER 12: BE A GREAT ENTREPRENEUR

1 – Driven

1 https://www.linkedin.com/pulse/20140620185038-334219545-drive-determination-and-passion-three-keys-to-success-in-business-and-in-life 2 https://www.forbes.com/sites/ryanmac/2013/03/13/five-startup-lessons-from-gopro-founder-and-billionaire-nick-woodman/#5ab9b85e546e

3 https://www.forentrepreneurs.com/what-drives-great-entrepreneurs/

2 – Enthusiasm

1 https://www.forbes.com/profile/elon-musk/

2 "Western Union's Bad Call on the Telephone." National Geographic 100 Shocking Events Disasters, Scandals, and Misadventures That Made History. Jan. 2017 p. 10.

3 https://www.britannica.com/biography/Walter-P-Chrysler

3 – Taking Initiative

1 https://www.history.com/this-day-in-history/ford-celebrates-1-millionth-mustang

2 https://wheels.blogs.nytimes.com/2009/07/10/mustang-vs-camaro-wasnt-much-of-a-battle

3 https://www.juliusbaer.com/global/en/news-insights/news-insights-detail-page/item/first-movers-how-to-make-the-most-of-an-early-advantage/

4 https://www.quora.com/What-are-the-examples-of-First-mover-advantage-in-Startups

4 – Focus

1 https://medium.com/swlh/how-to-unlock-the-true-potential-of-your-business-7129277034d

2 https://www.entrepreneur.com/article/244742

3 https://www.entrepreneur.com/article/239096

4 https://www.prnewswire.com/news-releases/just-say-no-narrow-companys-vision-to-boost-all-stakeholders-204458411.html

5 https://www.entrepreneur.com/slideshow/286302#3

5 – Leadership

1 https://www.investors.com/news/management/leaders-and-success/jack-welch-built-ge-success-on-continuous-learning/

2 https://www.mckinsey.com/business-functions/strategy-and-corporate-finance/our-insights/ten-tips-for-leading-companies-out-of-crisis

Endnotes

6 – Persistence

1 http://www.businessinsider.com/vc-martin-casado-advice-grads-get-good-at-failure-2017-5

2 https://www.forbes.com/sites/neilpatel/2015/01/16/90-of-startups-will-fail-heres-what-you-need-to-know-about-the-10/#ad67e1666792

3 https://www.fastcompany.com/1638838/persistence-key-success

4 http://www.smbceo.com/2017/06/13/the-importance-of-persistence-in-business/

7 – Risk Takers

1 https://in-business.org.uk/most-important-characteristics-of-an-entrepreneur/

2 https://www.huffingtonpost.com/2013/08/13/seven-reasons-why-risk-taking-leads-to-success_n_3749425.html

3 https://www.business.com/images/content/58a/d9f1f2f87b1207f720c3d/0-0-/

4 https://www.liveplan.com/blog/2017/02/why-risk-takers-are-winners-and-why-all-entrepreneurs-should-take-risks/

8 – Self-Confidence

1 https://www.macworld.co.uk/feature/apple/history-of-apple-steve-jobs-mac-3606104/

9 – Team Builders

1 history.com/this-day-in-history/fords-assembly-line-starts-rolling

2 https://en.wikipedia.org/wiki/List_of_wealthiest_historical_figures

3 https://www.inc.com/drew-hendricks/10-habits-of-the-successful-entrepreneur.html

4 https://www.entrepreneur.com/article/305418

5 https://www.forbes.com/sites/alanhall/2013/05/03/12-characteristics-of-wildly-successful-entrepreneurs/#2df63675147a

10 – Smart

1 https://en.wikipedia.org/wiki/Bill_Gates

2 https://en.wikipedia.org/wiki/Elizabeth_Holmes and https://www.businessinsider.com/theranos-lays-off-about-100-employees-2018-4

Additional Training

Sean has further training available at

WorldsGreatestBusinessPlan.com

as well as

Training.SeanCastrina.com

About the Author

EQUIPPING ENTREPRENEURS FOR SUCCESS

Sean Castrina is the bestselling author of The Greatest Entrepreneur in the World and 8 Unbreakable Rules for Business Startup Success. He has contributed to some of the most recognized media outlets including Forbes, Inc., Money, as well as guest lectured at some of America's finest colleges.

He is a serial entrepreneur having started more than 20 companies and currently is an active C.E.O. He is the host of one of iTunes most listened to business podcasts, The Ten Minute Entrepreneur.

Visit SeanCastrina.com
for more essential business tips!

Made in the USA
Monee, IL
04 November 2026

67387234R00085